PLAY LIKE LAMINE

GROW YOUR GAME:
CONFIDENCE, SMARTS, AND SKILL

PLAY LIKE LAMINE
Grow Your Game: Confidence, Smarts, and Skill

Published by Sole Books
PO Box 10445
Beverly Hills, CA 90213
United States

For bulk orders, translation rights, or licensing inquiries: *info@solebooks.com*

ISBN: 9781938591518

Cover design: Mirko Pohle
Interior design: Lazar Kackarovski

Printed in the United States of America
First Edition: March 2026

The exercises and training suggestions in this book are intended for educational purposes. Readers should practice safely and under appropriate supervision.

www.solebooks.com

PLAY LIKE Lamine

GROW YOUR GAME:
CONFIDENCE, SMARTS, AND SKILL

STEVE BERG & NOAH VIDAL

A NOTE FROM THE AUTHOR

To the Smallest Player on the Field

If you are reading this, there's a good chance you've been told you are "too small," "too skinny," or that you need to wait for a growth spurt before you can truly compete.

Maybe you've felt the shadow of a defender twice your size. Maybe you've felt your heart race when the game gets fast and loud. Maybe you've wondered if you have what it takes to survive in a game that often feels like it belongs to the giants.

This book was written for you.

Lamine Yamal didn't become a world-class Number 10 because he was the strongest person on the pitch. He didn't do it by being a giant. He did it by being fearless.

Lamine proved to the world that when you have a "skinny" frame, you have a secret weapon: speed of thought. While others are trying to use their muscles, you are going to use your mind. While they are trying to be loud, you are going to be precise.

We are going to study the inner game—the part of soccer that happens inside your chest and behind your eyes. You will learn:

- **How to find calm when everyone else is panicking.**
- **How to use fearless simplicity to outsmart the biggest defenders.**
- **How to build an inner confidence that no growth spurt can give you.**

To the parents reading this: You aren't just raising an athlete; you are raising a person. This book is designed to help your child find the courage to be themselves on and off the field.

Soccer is a game of feet, but greatness is a game of the spirit.

Welcome to the series. Welcome to your new mindset.

Let's play.

FOREWORD

The Academy of Total Soccer

When Lamine Yamal was just three years old, soccer was just a ball, a dusty street, and the most exciting thing in the world.

In his neighborhood of Rocafonda, in Barcelona, Spain, games didn't start with a referee's whistle. They started when a ball hit the pavement and someone shouted, "Next goal wins!" There were no painted lines or official jerseys. No parents filming on their phones. No coaches with clipboards. Just kids, trash cans for goalposts, and the frantic magic of the chase.

When Lamine played with older kids, he noticed something early: if he tried to wrestle the big kids for the ball, he would lose. He had to be different.

He learned to control the ball with a soft touch so it never left his side.

This same idea was born years earlier from a man named Johan Cruyff.

Cruyff was a legendary player for FC Barcelona and the Netherlands. When he was young, people said he was too skinny. He proved them wrong. When he became a coach, he didn't care if a player was the tallest or the strongest. He said:

> **"You play soccer with your head, and your legs are there to help you."**

He believed that if you keep the ball, the other team can't hurt you—even if you are smaller. It doesn't matter if the opponent is twice your size. If they can't touch the ball, they can't win. To keep the ball, you must develop control and the ability to make precise passes in tight spaces.

There was another idea: Total Soccer. A player wasn't only a defender, midfielder, or forward. Everyone learned to move and think in every position.

For a player like Lamine, this was perfect. He wasn't stuck in one spot where big defenders could trap him. He could pop up anywhere, like a ghost, moving the ball before anyone could catch him.

Cruyff also said that "speed" isn't just about running fast. It's about starting earlier because you saw the play before anyone else.

Lamine was learning to see the future.

This is what Tiki-Taka is about. The name sounds like the "tick-tock" of a clock because the ball moves quickly—pass, pass, pass—until the other team is chasing shadows.

This is why Lionel Messi was a perfect fit for La Masia. Small and not the strongest on the pitch, he became one of the greatest players of all time.

CHAPTER 1

LA MASIA

Lamine's Second Home

At age six, Lamine was accepted to La Masia. A scout saw his talent, and the academy welcomed him in a move that changed his life. La Masia and Lamine were a perfect fit. It was time to shape his raw street talent and help him grow as both a player and a person.

THE LAMINE RULE

Use your head before you use your legs.

Soccer is where thinking about the game and **your** role in it makes a huge difference. The game is played when you don't have the ball. Knowing what to do without the ball is the most important thing you should learn.

- Look for pockets of space where the opponent can't reach you.
- Find an open teammate before you even receive the ball.

LEARNING AND LIVING AT LA MASIA

La Masia is a place where kids train, and many live together.

HOW LIFE WORKS AT THE ACADEMY

- ✔ School Comes First: You aren't just a soccer player. You are a student.
- ✔ Kindness Is Key: Being a good person matters more than winning a trophy.
- ✔ Ask Questions: Coaches ask questions so you learn to solve the puzzle yourself.

- ✔ **Lionel Messi**
  Small, quiet, unstoppable.
- ✔ **Xavi Hernández**
  Master of the perfect pass.
- ✔ **Andrés Iniesta**
  Calm in the biggest moments.
- ✔ **Sergio Busquets**
  Always in the right place.

Those players were small in size but had great control over their bodies and the ball. Above all, they were thinking fast. Their skill and intelligence win games.

WHAT LAMINE LEARNED

Treat the ball as if it's your best friend.

TRY THIS

The Close Control Challenge

Find a small space—even a hallway works.

- **Play** for 10 minutes without keeping score.
- **Count** how many controlled touches you make without hitting an obstacle.
- **Use** the inside and outside of your foot. Keep your knees slightly bent.

THINK LIKE A PLAYER

- How do you react when someone is better than you?
- Do you learn more when you lose or when you win?
- What makes soccer fun for you?

WORDS TO REMEMBER

"When you understand the game, the game slows down."

COACH'S WISDOM

All great players have something in common. They loved the game passionately. They dreamed about it. They played at every opportunity. That love started early. Keeping this love and excitement as you grow is vital.

In Catalan, La Masia means "the farmhouse." The academy began in a real farmhouse built in the 1700s.

CHAPTER 2

TOUCH BEFORE YOU RUSH

The Wild Ball

At an early age, soccer isn't about positions or formations. It's about the first touch. The ball can feel wild. It rolls away faster than you expect or bounces when you don't want it to. That's normal. The best young players aren't the ones who kick the hardest. They're the ones who stay close to the ball and treat it with care.

Lamine didn't smash the ball forward every time he got it. He took one touch, then another. He placed his foot gently on top of the ball to quiet it. He let it settle—and only then decided what to do next.

He learned that kind of patience was a superpower.

Touch Comes Before Speed

Between ages six and eight, soccer is about learning how the ball reacts to you. This is the "feeling stage," where you learn:

- The Egg Catch: Stop the ball gently, like catching an egg.
- The Glue: Keep the ball close while moving.
- The Pivot: Turn without losing control.

THE LAMINE RULE

"If the ball listens to you, the game becomes easier."

In soccer, you don't fight the ball—you guide it. Lamine's secret was patience. When the ball stays within one step of your feet, you stay in control.

Strength and speed will come later. Comfort with the ball starts now. At La Masia, young players spend hours simply touching the ball. Not shooting. Not crossing. Just feeling it.

Small Spaces Make Smart Players

Big fields can hide mistakes. Small spaces can't.

When you play in a tight area—like a hallway or backyard:

- **You touch the ball more often.**
- **You think faster.**
- **You learn the three C's: Control, Creativity, Calm.**

Lamine didn't need a perfect pitch. He needed a ball—and the freedom to try again.

Losing the Ball Is Part of the Game

Young players lose the ball often. That's not failure—that's data. Your brain is learning what doesn't work so it can discover what does.

The real question isn't, "Did I lose the ball?"

It's, "What did I do next?"

Lamine didn't freeze or complain. He stayed involved. That habit matters more than scoring goals.

Keep the Ball Close

If you remember one thing from this chapter, remember this:

A close ball gives you time to think.

- When the ball is close: You can turn, pass, or surprise a defender.
- When the ball is far: You chase. You panic. You lose options.

Great players don't chase the ball. They invite it to stay.

WHAT LAMINE LEARNED

- ✔ The ball is your partner, not your enemy.
- ✔ Gentle touches beat strong kicks.
- ✔ Small spaces are the best teachers.
- ✔ Comfort comes before speed.

TRY THIS

The "Ball Friend" Challenge

- ✔ ***Goal:*** Keep the ball within one step at all times.
- ✔ ***Rule:*** Walk, don't run. Turn slowly. Use both feet.
- ✔ ***Level 2:*** Use only the inside of your foot for one minute, then only the outside.

THINK LIKE A PLAYER

- Does the ball stay close to me, or am I chasing it?
- Do I rush passes because I'm nervous?
- Which foot feels more comfortable—and how can I strengthen the other?

WORDS TO REMEMBER

"The ball should feel like it belongs to you."

COACH'S WISDOM

You don't need to sprint to be dangerous. Sometimes you slow down so you can see your next move. Play slow to see the game. Play fast to finish it.

What Does Lamine's Celebration Mean?

After scoring, Lamine sometimes forms the numbers 3-0-4 with his fingers. The number 304 represents the last three digits of Rocafonda's postal code—the neighborhood where he first learned to play. He never forgets where he came from.

CHAPTER 3

PLAY WITH YOUR EYES

Between ages eight and ten, soccer adds a new layer. The ball still matters—but now, so does everything around it.

Players begin to notice:

- **Teammates moving into open lanes.**
- **Opponents closing in from behind.**
- **Space opening up—then disappearing in a second.**

Most kids don't see this yet. They look down at their feet. They chase the ball. They react too late. But some players start lifting their heads before the ball even reaches them.

Lamine was one of them.

Before the ball arrived, he was already watching. Not staring—scanning. A quick look over his shoulder. Then another. When the ball came, he didn't panic. He already knew what he wanted to do.

From Touching to Thinking

This is when the game becomes a thinking game. You don't need to be faster than everyone else—you need to see sooner.

THE LAMINE RULE

"Scan early. Decide early."

Your eyes are as important as your feet.

At La Masia, coaches don't say, "Pass there." They ask, "What did you see?"

When you scan early, the game feels slower. You aren't surprised—you're prepared.

The Power of the Shoulder Check

The best habit to learn at this age is the shoulder check—one quick glance over your shoulder before the ball arrives.

It tells you:

- ✔ Who is free for a pass.
- ✔ Who is about to tackle you.
- ✔ Where the "green grass" (open space) is.

That one look can save you two extra touches.

If you know where you're going before the ball reaches your foot, you don't have to stop, look, and then move. You can just go.

Lamine learned this early, and it made the game easier—and more fun.

Passing Is Not Giving the Ball Away

Many young players think passing means losing control. But passing is a secret weapon. It allows you to:

- Move the ball faster than anyone can run.
- Create space to receive it again in a better position.
- Keep the whole team connected.

Lamine didn't pass because he was afraid to dribble. He passed because he trusted his teammates.

And once the ball left his foot, he didn't stop. He moved immediately—staying connected to the play like an invisible string tied him to the ball.

First Decisions Matter Most

You don't need perfect decisions. You need clear ones.

At this age, the first option you see is often the best one.

- ✔ **Trust your gut:** If you see a teammate open, pass.
- ✔ **Don't hesitate:** Hesitation gives defenders time.
- ✔ **Keep it simple:** Simple soccer is fast soccer.

WHAT LAMINE LEARNED

- ✔ Looking up changes everything.
- ✔ Seeing early creates "extra time" in your mind.
- ✔ The ball moves faster than legs ever will.

- ✔ A quick shoulder check is like having a map of the field.
- ✔ Moving after you pass makes you harder to guard.
- ✔ Thinking early keeps you calm under pressure.

TRY THIS

The "Awareness" Challenge

You can practice "seeing" even when you're alone:

The Solo Scan

- Stand with a ball facing a wall or curb.
- Before kicking the ball, look over your shoulder and spot a specific color (a red car, blue chair, or green leaf).
- Kick the ball. As it comes back, scan again for a different color before touching it.

The Partner Game

- Have a friend stand behind you.
- As the ball rolls toward you, they hold up a number of fingers.
- You must shout out the number before touching the ball.

THINK LIKE A PLAYER

- Did I look over my shoulder before the ball reached me?
- Did I know where my teammates were before receiving the ball?
- Did I move into a new space right after I passed?

WORDS TO REMEMBER

"You can't play what you don't see."

COACH'S WISDOM

The game opens up when you look up early.

Imagine you are a photographer. If you only look at your feet, you miss the whole picture. When you lift your head, you see a much wider picture.

Great players aren't just athletes. They see the game as a movie—because it's always moving.

Two Meetings with a Legend

Lamine's journey with Lionel Messi feels like something out of a movie. They met twice long before Lamine became a star.

The Bath-Time Photo

When Lamine was six months old, his mother won a draw to participate in an FC Barcelona photoshoot for UNICEF, which cares for children in need. The player assigned to pose with him? A young Lionel Messi. There is a famous photo of Messi helping bathe baby Lamine—a moment many fans now see as symbolic.

The Tunnel Walk

Years later, as a student at La Masia, Lamine was chosen as a mascot for a match at Camp Nou. Photographers captured Messi holding young Lamine's hand as they walked out of the tunnel together.

CHAPTER 4

THE TEN TEAMMATES WHO TRUST YOU

Around age ten, something important changes. The field feels bigger. There are more players. Suddenly, you're not just playing near others—you're playing with them.

This is when soccer stops being about what you can do alone and starts becoming about what you can create together.

Some players struggle here. They want the ball all the time. They dribble too long. They forget their teammates exist.

Lamine noticed something different early on.

When he shared the ball, he often received it back—in a better position.

That discovery changed everything.

Space Becomes Real

You start to learn:

- ✔ Spreading Out: Standing too close to a teammate makes it easy for one defender to guard both of you.
- ✔ Creating Options: Moving away from the ball can give your teammate more room.
- ✔ The Invisible Work: Moving without the ball is real work. You don't need to touch it to help the team.

At La Masia, players hear one rule again and again:

"Make the field big when you have the ball."

THE LAMINE RULE

Passing is a conversation.

Passing isn't just kicking the ball away. It's starting a conversation with your feet.

You pass to say:

- ✔ **"I see you."**
- ✔ **"I trust you."**
- ✔ **"Now it's your turn."**

And like any real conversation, it doesn't end when you speak. You move. You offer yourself again. You stay connected.

Soccer flows best when players never stop "talking."

Trust Makes the Game Easier

When you trust your teammates:

- **You don't panic under pressure.**
- **You don't rush decisions.**
- **You don't try to do everything alone.**

At La Masia, players learn that no one wins alone. Even the most talented players depend on their team.

Lamine didn't try to be the hero every time he touched the ball. He trusted the group—and because of that, the group trusted him back.

WHAT LAMINE LEARNED

- ✔ Passing to a teammate is often the best way to keep the ball.
- ✔ Creating space for others is a superpower.
- ✔ A team that trusts one another plays faster.
- ✔ You are still playing—even when the ball is far from you.
- ✔ Teams beat individuals.

TRY THIS

The "*Give-and-Go*" Challenge

Play with one or two friends.

- ***Goal:*** Don't count goals—count connections.
- ***Rule:*** Two-touch maximum. Move to a new spot immediately after every pass.

- ***Challenge:*** Complete 10 passes in a row without the ball stopping or a defender touching it.

THINK LIKE A PLAYER

- Am I helping my team even when I don't have the ball?
- Do I stand still after I pass—or do I search for new space?
- Do I trust my teammates enough to pass in tight moments?

WORDS TO REMEMBER

"Soccer is played together—or not at all."

COACH'S WISDOM

When you share the ball, the game opens.

Think of a puzzle. If you hold all the pieces, no one sees the picture. When everyone adds their piece, the full image—the goal—appears.

The Rise to the Prize

Lamine's journey to Barcelona's first team was record-breaking.

- The Debut: On April 29, 2023, coach Xavi named Lamine to the bench. He was just 15 years and 290 days old.
- The Record: He entered the match against Real Betis in the 83rd minute, becoming the youngest player to appear for Barcelona's first team in La Liga.
- The Numbers: In that first game, he wore jersey number 41. Later he was given number 27—and eventually the famous number 19 for both Spain and Barcelona.
- The Prized 10: In the 2025–2026 season, Lamine was awarded the iconic number 10—the shirt worn by legends like Ronaldinho and Lionel Messi. He didn't just receive the number; he earned the trust that comes with it.

CHAPTER 5

CONTROL. PASS. SCORE.

When Lamine scores, people talk about the finish.

The goal.

The angle.

The celebration.

But the magic doesn't start there.

It starts earlier.

With a touch that moves the ball into space.

With a pass that arrives at the perfect speed.

With a decision that makes the final action feel simple.

Lamine doesn't rush goals.

He builds them.

The First Touch Is the Real Move

Lamine's first touch is rarely flashy.

But it is always intentional.

He doesn't just stop the ball.

He directs it.

His first touch usually:

- **Moves the ball away from pressure**
- **Sets up the next action**
- **Buys him time**

That's why defenders are often late—before they even try to defend him.

A clean first touch gives you something special:

Time.

And time makes soccer feel slower.

THE LAMINE RULE

Your first touch should make the next play easier.

Correct Is Better Than Hard

Lamine's passes aren't about power.

They're about weight.

A correct pass:

- **Reaches your teammate's strong foot**
- **Is easy to control**
- **Allows the next play to happen quickly**

Hard passes can slow the game.

Correct passes speed it up.

Lamine passes so his teammates don't have to adjust or struggle.

That's why they trust him.

And that's why the ball keeps coming back.

Move After You Pass

Passing isn't the end of the play.

It's the beginning.

Lamine never passes and watches.

After passing, he:

- Changes position
- Finds a new angle
- Prepares for the return

Passing isn't giving the ball away.

It's investing in the next moment.

Composure Beats Power

When Lamine finishes, he rarely looks rushed.

Even close to goal, he stays balanced.

That allows him to:

- Place the ball instead of smashing it
- Choose a corner
- Adjust at the last second

Great scorers don't panic.

They arrive composed and ready.

- Clean control
- Smart movement
- Early decisions

And scoring becomes easier.

WHAT LAMINE LEARNED

- ✔ First touch creates time.
- ✔ Correct passes build trust.
- ✔ Moving after you pass creates chances.
- ✔ Composure opens space.
- ✔ Goals start before the shot.

TRY THIS

The Lamine Circuit

Part 1 — Control

- Pass against a wall.
- First touch moves the ball sideways.
- Second touch passes it back.

Part 2 — Passing

- Pass to a partner.
- Aim for their front foot.
- Use the correct speed.

Part 3 — Finish

- Receive a soft pass.
- One touch to set.
- One focused shot.

Do it slowly.

Clean beats fast.

THINK LIKE A PLAYER

- Did my first touch help me?
- Was my pass easy to control?
- Did I move after passing?
- Was I calm when I finished?

WORDS TO REMEMBER

"Good control makes the game feel slower."

COACH'S WISDOM

Goals come from control—not chaos.

If your touch is clean, your pass is correct, and your movement is smart, the finish becomes simple.

Don't chase goals.

Build them.

Many of Lamine's goals and assists come after only one or two touches.

He doesn't need five moves.

His earlier decisions already did the work.

CHAPTER 6

TRAIN YOUR BRAIN

Around ages eleven and twelve, the game shifts gears.

Not because everyone suddenly becomes faster—but because the game begins to repeat itself.

There is less space, less time, and more pressure. But something else changes too: patterns appear. The same defensive movements. The same passing lanes. The same mistakes.

Some players panic when space disappears. They kick the ball away just to feel safe.

Lamine noticed something different. When he recognized the pattern early, the pressure didn't surprise him. He wasn't reacting—he was anticipating.

As the game sped up, his reading of it became his greatest skill.

When Pressure Arrives

At this age, you'll notice three big changes:

- No Space: Opponents close you down instantly.
- High Stakes: One mistake can lead to a goal.
- Bigger Expectations: Coaches expect quicker decisions.

Smart players don't try to outrun pressure—they learn to recognize it before it fully arrives.

At La Masia, players often hear:

> **"You don't need more time.**
> **You need better timing."**

Timing comes from seeing what others miss.

Reading the Clues

Fast thinking is not rushing.

Fast thinking is recognizing what is about to happen.

Good players begin to notice small clues:

- A defender leaning too far forward before tackling.
- A teammate starting a run before calling for the ball.
- A passing lane that will close in one second.
- A goalkeeper shifting weight before a shot.

Lamine was trained to notice these details. By the time the ball reached him, he wasn't guessing—he was confirming what he already understood.

That's why he looks calm when others look frantic.

He has already solved the problem in his mind.

THE LAMINE RULE

See the problem before it becomes pressure.

If you recognize the situation early, you don't feel rushed later.

When you've faced the same situation many times in practice, your brain stops treating it like danger. It becomes information instead of fear.

When a defender charges:

- **Breathe.**
- **Trust what you recognized.**
- **Act clearly—not emotionally.**

The more patterns you recognize, the slower the game feels.

Decisions in a Heartbeat

Often you have the ball, or you're moving into space, and you aren't sure what to do.

Hesitation is often the real mistake.

An early, clear decision is usually better than a late one. When you hesitate, everyone on the field reacts—your teammates and your opponents. You may miss a window that was open for only a second.

Lamine doesn't wait for the "perfect" option. He chooses the best available one and commits.

That commitment makes his movements look confident.

Even when he's wrong, he is decisive.

And decisive players recover faster than hesitant ones.

WHAT LAMINE LEARNED

- ✔ Pressure repeats itself.
- ✔ Early recognition beats late reaction.
- ✔ Small clues reveal big opportunities.
- ✔ Decisive players control tempo.

TRY THIS

The "Pattern Spotter" Challenge

Play a short game with friends.

- Before receiving the ball, quickly name one thing you notice (a teammate's run, a defender's position, open space).
- After the game, ask yourself: What situations kept repeating?
- Next time you play, look for those patterns earlier.

The goal is not to move faster.

It's to see sooner.

THINK LIKE A PLAYER

- Did I recognize pressure before it fully arrived?
- What clues did I notice before receiving the ball?
- Do I react—or do I anticipate?
- When did I hesitate? Why?

WORDS TO REMEMBER

"Quick decisions give you time to find better options."

COACH'S WISDOM

Great players don't just play the moment—they predict it.

Think of chess. The best players aren't reacting to the current move. They're already thinking two moves ahead.

Soccer works the same way.

Train your eyes.

Train your brain.

The body will follow.

The History-Maker in Berlin

Lamine Yamal rewrote the record books at Euro 2024.

- The Record: At 16 years and 362 days old, he became the youngest goalscorer in European Championship history.
- The Birthday Moment: He turned 17 one day before the final—and helped Spain lift the trophy while winning the Young Player of the Tournament award.

His talent was visible.

But what stood out most was how composed he looked on the biggest stage.

He had seen the patterns before.

CHAPTER 7

ARE YOU THAT GOOD?

Around ages twelve and thirteen, something new appears: attention.

People start noticing who is talented. Coaches talk more. Parents talk more. Teammates talk more. Compliments arrive—but so do expectations.

Some players change when this happens. They show off. They stop listening. They begin playing for praise instead of playing for the game.

Lamine heard the noise—but he didn't let it change him. He stayed the same player: calm, focused, respectful.

That wasn't luck. It was a choice.

Confidence Gets Tested

At this age, you know you're good—and others know it too. This is when confidence can turn into ego—or into something much stronger.

True confidence doesn't shout. It doesn't demand the ball or search for cameras.

At La Masia, players are reminded:

> **"Talent opens doors.**
> **Behavior decides how long you stay."**

Confidence vs. Ego

It's important to know the difference.

- Confidence says: "I trust my ability. I'll try again. I can learn from this mistake."
- Ego says: "I'm better than them. Give me the ball so I can shine. It's not my fault we lost."

Lamine didn't play to prove he was special. He played to help the team win.

Confidence makes you brave enough to try a difficult pass.

Ego makes you fragile—because you become afraid to fail in front of others.

THE LAMINE RULE

Humility makes you a better player.

Respect Is a Skill

Respect isn't just about being nice. It's part of high-level soccer.

Respect means:

- ✔ Listening to your coach.
- ✔ Helping a struggling teammate.
- ✔ Taking every opponent seriously.

Lamine respected the game. And because he respected it, the game gave him its secrets.

At La Masia, respect is trained like dribbling or passing. It isn't optional.

Learning From Better Players

At this age, you will meet players who are better—older, stronger, faster.

Some players feel threatened. Smart players feel curious.

Lamine didn't feel small around older stars. He watched them.

He didn't just copy their tricks. He studied their habits—how they moved without the ball, how they stayed calm under pressure.

Smart players steal ideas—not attention.

WHAT LAMINE LEARNED

- ✔ Confidence grows from preparation, not praise.
- ✔ Ego blocks your ears—and you can't learn if you don't listen.
- ✔ Respect earns trust.
- ✔ Every great player is a teacher in disguise.
- ✔ Staying grounded keeps you ready to grow.

TRY THIS

Silent Training

Try this in a short practice game with friends.

- **Rule:** No talking. No complaining. No loud celebrations.
- **Focus:** Communicate with movement, eye contact, and decisions.
- **Goal:** Notice how much more you see when you aren't busy speaking.

After the game, ask yourself: Did silence make you calmer—or frustrated?

THINK LIKE A PLAYER

- How do I react when someone praises me?
- Do I listen to corrections—or make excuses?
- Am I playing to look good—or to make the team better?

WORDS TO REMEMBER

"Confidence is quiet. Ego is loud."

COACH'S WISDOM

The strongest players stay humble.

Think of a bridge. It doesn't announce how strong it is—it simply carries the weight.

Be the player your teammates can rely on. Your game will speak for you.

A Heart of Many Colors

Lamine Yamal represents Spain—but his roots stretch far beyond one country.

- The Choice: Because of his parents, Lamine was eligible to play for three national teams: Spain (his birthplace), Morocco (his father's home), and Equatorial Guinea (his mother's home).
- The Decision: After Morocco's historic 2022 World Cup run, they strongly encouraged him to join. But Lamine had grown up in Spain's youth system and felt deeply connected to the red jersey.
- The Tribute: Even while playing for Spain, he honors his heritage. His cleats often feature the flags of Morocco and Equatorial Guinea. He also returns to Rocafonda to stay connected to the community that shaped him.

Staying grounded is part of his strength.

CHAPTER 8

WINNING ISN'T EVERYTHING

At ages thirteen and fourteen, mistakes feel heavier.

Games are more serious. Opponents are smarter. Sidelines are louder. One bad touch can feel like a disaster. One lost ball can feel embarrassing.

This is when many players change how they play. They stop trying new things and choose "safe" moves instead of courageous ones.

Lamine did the opposite.

When a move didn't work, he didn't hide. He didn't stare at the ground. He asked for the ball again.

That's the only way creativity survives.

Fear Tries to Enter

Between ages thirteen and fourteen, expectations rise—and every mistake gets noticed. Pressure becomes real.

This is the age when players either:

- **Play not to lose (play scared).**
- **Play to learn (play brave).**

At La Masia, players hear a powerful idea:

"Mistakes are information."

A mistake isn't a stop sign. It's a message telling you what to adjust next time.

What Mistakes Actually Teach

Every mistake answers a question you didn't know you had:

- **Was the space really there?**
- **Was my timing right?**
- **Was my decision clear?**

Lamine didn't argue with his mistakes. He didn't get angry at himself.

He listened.

He adjusted—lighter touch, earlier pass, or waiting half a second longer.

That's how players grow without fear.

THE LAMINE RULE

A mistake is a lesson in disguise.

Why Trying Again Matters

The most important moment in a game isn't the mistake—it's the next moment.

Do you hide?

Or do you ask for the ball again?

Lamine always asked for it.

Not because he never felt pressure—but because he trusted is fellow students and coaches.

Creativity needs safety. That safety comes from knowing one mistake won't define you.

Courage Beats Perfection

Perfect soccer doesn't exist—not even for the best players in the world.

Creative soccer does.

At this age, the players who stand out are the ones who:

- ✔ Try difficult things.
- ✔ Learn from what went wrong.
- ✔ Don't repeat the same mistake twice.

Lamine learned from mistakes.

He repeated courage.

WHAT LAMINE LEARNED

- ✔ Mistakes are feedback, not failure.
- ✔ Fear is what truly slows you down.
- ✔ Asking for the ball again builds trust.
- ✔ Creativity requires risk.
- ✔ Growth matters more than perfection.

TRY THIS

The Risk Round

Next time you play a short game:

- ***Rule:*** Every player must attempt one risky move (a difficult pass, a new turn, or a long shot).
- ***Atmosphere:*** No complaining if it fails.
- ***Goal:*** After the game, discuss what worked and what didn't. Focus on learning—not the score.

THINK LIKE A PLAYER

- How do I react in the first ten seconds after losing the ball?
- Do I stop calling for it during a "bad" game?
- What did my last mistake teach me?
- Am I playing to be perfect—or to improve?

WORDS TO REMEMBER

"You can't create without risking."

COACH'S WISDOM

Mistakes don't stop you—fear does.

Think of a scientist in a lab. If an experiment fails, they don't quit. They write down what happened and try again.

You are a soccer scientist.

Every time the ball rolls away, you've discovered one way that didn't work. Now go find the one that does.

Family First

Even as Lamine became one of the most famous teenagers in the world, he stayed close to the people who were there before the big stadiums.

- The Cousin: Lamine's cousin, Mohamed Abde, supported him from the beginning. Before Lamine could drive himself to training, his family—including Abde—made sure he arrived on time.

Staying connected keeps him grounded.

CHAPTER 9

SPACE IS OPPORTUNITY

When you watch soccer on TV or in a stadium, you are seeing a different game than the one players like Lamine see.

They see gaps. Moments. Tiny windows that open—and close—in seconds.

Often, the most important move happens before the ball even arrives. Lamine learned early that where he stood could make the next pass look easy—or impossible.

What Space Really Means

Space isn't just empty grass. It's opportunity.

Space exists between defenders, behind them, beside them—and sometimes right in front of them.

Good players don't chase the ball. They position themselves so the ball can find them.

At La Masia, players are taught a golden rule:

"Be where the game is going—not where it is."

Standing Still vs. Standing Smart

Many players think they must run constantly to help. But nonstop running can close space instead of creating it.

Sometimes, the smartest move is to:

- **Take two small steps sideways.**
- **Pause.**
- **Let the defender move first.**

Lamine doesn't waste energy. He waits in the right place.

That makes defenders nervous—because when you wait well, you can strike the moment the ball arrives.

THE LAMINE RULE

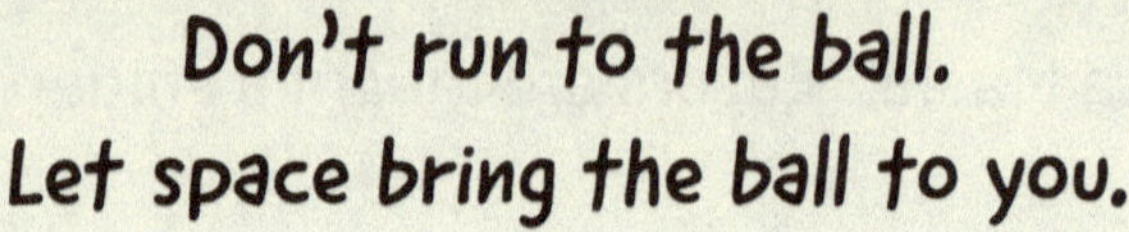

Don't run to the ball.
Let space bring the ball to you.

Finding the Pockets

A "pocket" is a small space between the opponent's midfield and defense. It isn't obvious—but it's powerful.

Lamine loves these pockets.

He slips into them quietly, receives the ball, turns, and creates danger.

Pockets disappear quickly. Timing matters more than raw speed.

Arrive too early, and the defender notices.

Arrive too late, and the window closes.

Arrive just in time—and you control the game.

Moving to Help Others

Your movement can help the team—even if you never touch the ball.

When you move with purpose:

✔ Defenders are forced to follow.
✔ Space opens for someone else.
✔ Teammates gain an extra second.

Lamine understands that movement is communication.

You don't need to shout. Your position speaks.

By dragging a defender away, you give your teammate a gift of space.

WHAT LAMINE LEARNED

✔ Space appears and disappears like a heartbeat.
✔ Positioning beats constant sprinting.
✔ Small movements are often the most dangerous.
✔ Pockets are where creativity begins.
✔ Your movement can unlock the defense for someone else.

TRY THIS

Shadow Movement

Practice with a friend.

- **Setup:** One player has the ball. The mover stands 10–15 steps away.
- **Goal:** The mover finds "windows" where they can clearly see the ball between imaginary defenders.
- **Rule:** No shouting "Pass!" Stay open using small adjustments.
- **Focus:** Wait for the right moment to "pop" into space.

THINK LIKE A PLAYER

- Where was the space before I moved?
- Did my run help the team—even without the ball?
- Am I positioned to see the whole field?
- Did I move with a plan—or just run?

WORDS TO REMEMBER

"Space is created—not given."

COACH'S WISDOM

The best positions make soccer look easy.

Think of a game of tag. If you run straight at someone, you get caught. If you stay just outside their vision, you stay free.

Find the defender's blind spot—and you will always be an option.

The Six-Year-Old Pioneer

La Masia usually prefers that young players who live nearby stay at home until they are older.

But for Lamine, the rules changed.

- The Commute: Traveling daily from Rocafonda to the academy was difficult for his family.
- The Exception: Because coaches recognized his rare talent and commitment, they made an unusual decision. At just six years old, Lamine became one of the youngest residents ever to move into the La Masia dorms.

Even early on, the academy saw something special.

CHAPTER 10

Playing Simple Is Playing Smart

Johan Cruyff once said:

"Playing soccer is very simple, but playing simple soccer is the hardest thing there is."

As players grow, something tempting appears: options.

You can dribble.

You can shoot.

You can try something spectacular.

And sometimes, you should.

But players like Lamine understand something deeper:

The smartest choice is often the clearest one.

Simple doesn't mean boring.

It means controlled.

When the game gets fast and crowded, clarity becomes your advantage.

While others are fighting the moment, the simple player is guiding it.

It's About Rhythm

Playing simple isn't about always passing backward or avoiding risk.

It's about controlling the rhythm of the game.

Sometimes the game needs speed.

Sometimes it needs calm.

Smart players feel that difference.

They know:

- When to move the ball quickly
- When to slow things down
- When to protect possession
- When to attack immediately

Lamine doesn't just play the game.

He manages it.

THE LAMINE RULE

**Control the rhythm,
and you control the game.**

One Touch When It's Clear

One-touch play is powerful—not because it's flashy, but because it's efficient.

One touch works best when:

- **You've already recognized the situation**
- **The pass is clean**
- **The next option is obvious**

One touch moves the game forward.

But only when the moment is right.

Two Touches When You Need Control

One touch speeds the game up.

Two touches give you balance.

Lamine never forces a one-touch pass just to look sharp.

Sometimes the smartest play is:

- **First touch to settle**
- **Second touch to choose**

That extra half-second can:

- **Pull a defender out of position**
- **Open a better passing lane**

- Calm a chaotic moment

The first touch prepares.

The second touch decides.

When to Dribble — and Why

Dribbling is not decoration.

It's a solution.

Lamine dribbles when:

- ✔ The defender is off balance
- ✔ Space opens directly in front of him
- ✔ A teammate's movement creates isolation

He doesn't dribble to impress.

He dribbles to change the shape of the defense.

If a pass is better, he passes.

If a pause is better, he pauses.

If a dribble is necessary, he goes.

The decision always comes first.

Managing Chaos

In tight matches, emotions rise.

The crowd gets loud.

The score gets close.

The pressure grows.

This is when simple soccer matters most.

If your team feels rushed:

- ✔ **Take two touches.**
- ✔ **Keep possession.**
- ✔ **Let teammates breathe.**

If the opponent is disorganized:

- ✔ **Move the ball quickly.**
- ✔ **Attack before they reset.**

The smartest players don't add chaos.

They remove it.

WHAT LAMINE LEARNED

- ✔ **Clarity beats complexity.**
- ✔ **Rhythm matters as much as speed.**
- ✔ **One touch moves the game.**
- ✔ **Two touches control it.**
- ✔ **Dribbling must solve a problem.**
- ✔ **Smart players manage the moment—not just the ball.**

TRY THIS

The Tempo Game

Play a small-sided match with friends.

- For five minutes, limit yourselves to one or two touches.
- For the next five minutes, focus on slowing the game down and keeping possession.
- Notice how the rhythm changes.

Ask yourself:

When did the game feel under control?

When did it feel rushed?

Learning to feel tempo is learning to lead.

THINK LIKE A PLAYER

- Did I choose the clearest option available?
- Did I speed up when the moment required it—or slow down?
- Did I overcomplicate a simple situation?
- When did I help my team breathe?

WORDS TO REMEMBER

"Simple soccer is smart soccer."

COACH'S WISDOM

The smartest move often looks easy.

Think of a master chef. They don't use twenty ingredients if three will make the perfect meal.

In soccer, don't use five touches if one will do.

Great players don't prove how much they can do.

They prove how little they need.

Passing the Torch

Do you remember the story from Chapter 3 about baby Lamine being held by Lionel Messi during a UNICEF photoshoot?

Years later, history echoed itself.

- The Recreation: After Lamine became a star, UNICEF invited him for a new photoshoot.
- The Big Brother: This time, Lamine held a baby—his own little brother, Keyne.
- The Circle: From being the child in Messi's arms to inspiring the next generation, Lamine became part of the story himself.

From the baby in the picture to the leader on the field, the rhythm continues.

CHAPTER 11

Training Off the Pitch

What You Do Away From the Ball Matters Too

Some players think training ends when the whistle blows. They put the ball away, forget about soccer, and hope they play well the next day.

But the greats understand something different:

How you live shapes how you play.

Lamine learned early that soccer didn't stop at the sideline. What he did at home, at school, and at night showed up in his game—slowly, over time.

The Hidden 23 Hours

At La Masia, players don't just train.

They live.

They study.

They rest.

They eat together.

Great players aren't built in one hour of practice.

They are built in the other 23.

Lamine was taught a simple truth:

Soccer is important—but it isn't your whole identity.

That balance protects players from burnout and keeps their love for the game alive.

Rest Is Training

Improvement doesn't only happen during practice.

It happens after.

When you rest:

- **Your body repairs itself.**
- **Your brain stores what you learned.**
- **Your focus returns sharper.**

Lamine treats rest as preparation.

Tired players react late.

Rested players react clearly.

School Builds Your Game

School isn't separate from soccer—it supports it.

The classroom teaches:

- **Focus — staying locked in**
- **Patience — solving hard problems**
- **Listening — understanding instructions**

At La Masia, education is mandatory. Even while becoming a global star, Lamine stayed serious about his studies.

Grounded players last longer.

Pressure Exists Off the Pitch Too

Some of the toughest challenges aren't defenders.

They are:

- **Social media**
- **Comparisons**
- **Expectations**

Learning to switch off matters.

By staying connected to family and real life, Lamine protected his freedom to play without fear.

THE LAMINE RULE

Your daily habits shape your game day.

WHAT LAMINE LEARNED

- ✔ Rest is preparation.
- ✔ Learning sharpens your thinking.
- ✔ Routines create stability.
- ✔ Balance protects confidence.
- ✔ Life fuels performance.

TRY THIS

The Weekly Balance Check

Once a week, ask yourself:

1. Did I get enough sleep?
2. Did I focus in school?
3. Did I eat food that helps me feel strong and healthy?
4. Did I enjoy something outside of soccer?

Write down one small thing to improve next week.

Small steps compound.

THINK LIKE A PLAYER

- Am I tired or prepared?
- Do my daily habits help my game?
- Am I balanced?
- What one routine can I improve this week?

WORDS TO REMEMBER

"Smart choices off the pitch make the game easier on it."

COACH'S WISDOM

Talent shines in games. Character is built before and after. It's in the hours no one sees—the effort, the discipline, and the choices you make.

The best players don't just train harder; they respect their body and mind away from the field—and it shows in every touch.

Homework at the Euros

During Euro 2024, while facing the world's best defenders, Lamine was also finishing his fourth year of high school.

He brought homework to the tournament. Between matches against Italy and Germany, he studied and completed online exams.

He even learned he had passed just before playing in the semi-finals.

You can be a superstar—and a serious student—at the same time.

CHAPTER 12

The Big Moments

Trust What You've Built

Big moments feel different.

Your heart beats faster.

Your legs feel heavier.

The crowd gets louder.

This is when some players disappear—and others arrive.

The difference isn't only talent. It's trust.

Lamine didn't perform in big moments by accident. He trusted the work he had done long before the stadium lights.

Pressure Is Normal

Pressure doesn't mean something is wrong.

It means something matters.

When you are older:

- Games feel bigger.
- More people are watching.
- Mistakes feel louder.

That feeling won't disappear. Strong players don't fight it—they use it.

At La Masia, players hear:

> **"Nerves mean you care. Use them."**

What Pressure Really Does

Pressure doesn't change your ability.

It tests your preparation.

Lamine doesn't try to be perfect in big games. He tries to be consistent.

He relies on:

- ✔ The same warm-up
- ✔ The same habits
- ✔ The same decisions

If you train honestly, big games begin to feel familiar.

Routines Create Stability

A routine makes a giant stadium feel manageable.

It can be:

- The way you warm up
- How you lace your cleats
- The first simple pass you look for

Small actions anchor your focus.

When the moment feels familiar, doubt loses its power.

Focus on the Next Action

Big moments don't require big ideas.

They require clear ones.

Ask yourself:

- What is my next action?
- Where is my teammate?
- How can I help right now?

Thinking only about the next touch keeps your mind steady—and a steady mind sees clearly.

THE LAMINE RULE

**Preparation builds belief.
Belief unlocks performance.**

TRY THIS

The 3-2-1 Reset

Before kickoff—or before a big moment:

1. Three slow breaths
2. Two quick scans
3. One clear first action

Know your first move.

The rest will follow.

WORDS TO REMEMBER

"Pressure reveals what you've practiced."

COACH'S WISDOM

Don't try to be a hero.

Be the player you prepared to be.

Consistency is louder than emotion.

The Miracle in Munich

In the Euro 2024 semi-final against France, Spain trailed 1–0.

At 16 years old, Lamine picked up the ball outside the box, looked up, and curled a shot into the top corner.

To the world, it looked like magic.

To Lamine, it was repetition meeting opportunity.

He had practiced that strike thousands of times.

Big moments reward quiet preparation.

CHAPTER 13

Growth Takes Time

Why Patience Is a Superpower

At some point, every young player compares.

- Who's taller?
- Who's stronger?
- Who scores more?

It's easy to feel behind.

But mastery doesn't grow in straight lines.

It grows in waves.

Lamine didn't arrive all at once—and neither will you.

Everyone Grows Differently

Some players grow early. Others grow later.

Some are fast at ten. Others find speed at fifteen.

Some discover their best position as adults.

At La Masia, players hear:

> **"Today's best player isn't always tomorrow's best player."**

Soccer rewards the patient player.

Quiet Progress

Improvement isn't always dramatic.

Sometimes it's:

- ✔ One better decision
- ✔ One steadier touch
- ✔ One smarter movement

They may not appear on the scoreboard—but they build your foundation.

Lamine trusted quiet progress.

Small improvements compound.

THE LAMINE RULE

- ✔ Development isn't a race.
- ✔ Everyone has a timeline.
- ✔ Persistence beats impatience.
- ✔ Small growth matters most.

THE TRAINING GROUND

The Progress Journal

Once a week, write:

1. One thing you improved
2. One thing you learned
3. One thing you enjoyed

No statistics.

Just growth.

WORDS TO REMEMBER

"Growth is happening—even when you can't see it."

COACH'S WISDOM

Great players are built slowly.

Talent is a seed. Character is the soil.

If you keep watering both, you'll outgrow those who relied only on size.

The Growth Spurt

When Lamine first joined Barcelona's academy, he was smaller than almost everyone in his age group.

Instead of worrying about height, he developed balance and a low center of gravity—just like Lionel Messi.

By the time he experienced a physical growth spurt at sixteen, his football intelligence was already advanced.

He didn't wait to grow bigger to play bigger.

CHAPTER 14

What Makes Lamine... Lamine

If you watch closely, you notice something.

He doesn't rush.

He doesn't force.

He doesn't panic.

Then suddenly—

A defender is wrong-footed.

A passing lane opens.

A chance appears.

That's style.

Not tricks.

Not noise.

Timing.

Style Is Decision-Making

Style isn't about highlight clips.

It's about choices.

- When to pass
- When to wait
- When to accelerate
- When to stop

Lamine doesn't play fast all the time.

He plays at the right time.

Timing Beats Speed

Speed is physical.

Timing is intelligence.

Lamine may not be the fastest player on the pitch—but he moves at the moment that matters.

He waits.

He watches.

He acts when the defender commits.

That's control.

Balance Changes Everything

Balance is physical—and mental.

Because Lamine stays balanced, he can:

- ✔ Dribble
- ✔ Pass
- ✔ Shoot
- ✔ Pause

All from the same position.

Balanced players give defenders no clues.

And uncertainty creates opportunity.

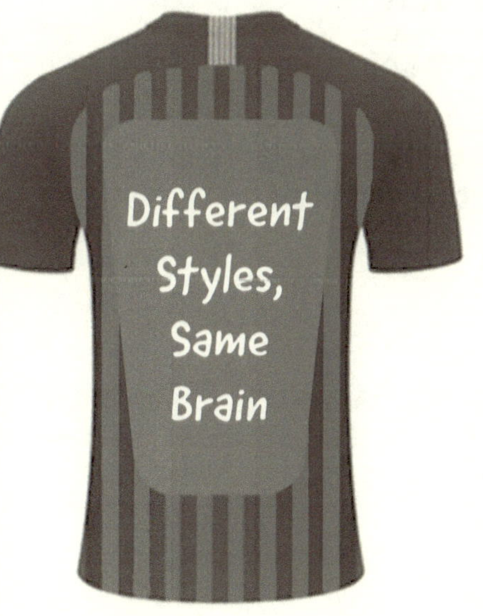

Great players look different—but think similarly.

- ✔ Pedri solves problems early.
- ✔ Cubarsí reads danger before it forms.
- ✔ Messi waited—then exploded.
- ✔ Busquets arrived first in his mind.

Different bodies.

Different roles.

Shared intelligence.

Lamine didn't copy their moves.

He studied how they think.

THE LAMINE RULE

Style is timing—not tricks.

WHAT MAKES HIS STYLE UNIQUE

- ✔ Steady under pressure
- ✔ Balanced in movement
- ✔ Precise in timing
- ✔ Courageous—but controlled
- ✔ Guided by rhythm

TRY THIS

The Timing Drill

Have a partner act as a defender.

1. Dribble slowly.
2. Wait for the defender to shift.
3. Then act.

Notice how patience makes everything easier.

WORDS TO REMEMBER

"Style is knowing when—not just how."

COACH'S WISDOM

Don't copy moves.

Copy thinking.

Under pressure, your real style appears.

The New Number 10

Lamine is a new kind of number 10. At Barça, he plays mainly on the right wing, combining vision, dribbling, and goal-scoring. He creates chances, scores from any range, and drifts across the pitch to surprise defenses. An all-around number 10!

In 2025, Lamine inherited Barcelona's legendary number 10 shirt.

The number once belonged to icons like Messi and Ronaldinho.

He didn't earn it with tricks.

He earned it with decisions.

Style isn't what you wear.

It's what you show.

CHAPTER 15

Playing Your Own Way

By now, you've learned the pillars:

- ✔ **Control**
- ✔ **Vision**
- ✔ **Composure**
- ✔ **Patience**

But there's something no coach can give you.

Your way of playing.

Lamine didn't become special by copying others. He learned from great players—then trusted his own instincts.

That's the final step.

There Is No Perfect Player

There is no perfect position.

No perfect path.

No perfect style.

Soccer needs every kind of player:

- **The creative dribbler**
- **The precise passer**
- **The quiet defender**
- **The vocal leader**

Trying to become someone else slows your growth.

Learning from others accelerates it.

Build Around Your Strengths

You don't need to master everything.

Find what comes naturally—calmness, vision, courage, discipline—and build from there.

Lamine built his game on balance and timing.

Your strengths may look different.

That's the point.

Joy Is the Fuel

When the game stops being joyful, something is off.

Joy isn't a reward.

It's energy.

- ✔ **Joy** keeps you curious.
- ✔ **Curiosity** keeps you learning.
- ✔ **Learning** keeps you growing.

Even with global expectations, Lamine never lost his connection to the ball.

That connection lasts longer than trophies.

You Are Allowed to Change

Your role will change.

Your body will change.

Your style will evolve.

That's development—not failure.

The player you are today is not the player you will be next year.

And that's a good thing.

THE LAMINE RULE

Be yourself—but keep building yourself.

WHAT THIS BOOK WAS REALLY ABOUT

- ✔ Thinking before acting
- ✔ Choosing clarity over chaos
- ✔ Managing pressure
- ✔ Growing patiently
- ✔ Playing with purpose
- ✔ Trusting your path

Smart players are built step by step.

TRY THIS

Your Player Statement

Write one sentence:

"The kind of player I am becoming is..."

Don’t write what sounds impressive.

Write what feels true.

Revisit it.

Adjust it.

Grow with it.

THINK LIKE A PLAYER

- What do I enjoy most?
- What am I proud of?
- What kind of teammate do I want to be?

WORDS TO REMEMBER

“The best players don’t copy—they own.”

COACH’S WISDOM

Great players aren’t built in one moment.

They are built in small choices every day.

One touch.

One decision.

One habit.

Identity grows quietly.

Where You Go From Here

Bring this book to training.

Choose one idea. Test it. Notice what changes.

Then choose another.

The field is still wide.

Your story is still being written.

And the next touch is yours.

THE MASTERCLASS

The La Masia Blueprint: Training the Barça Way

Now, it's time to put it into practice. To play like Lamine, you have to train like him. These are the five drills that every player at La Masia must master to become a "smart" player.

Five Essential Drills

If you want to play like a professional, you have to train like one. At La Masia, the ball is at the center of everything. These five drills aren't just about fitness—they are about teaching your brain to see the game before it happens.

1. The Classic Rondo (4v1 or 4v2)

This is the heartbeat of Barcelona. It looks like a simple game of "keep-away," but it is actually a high-speed lesson in geometry.

- **The Setup:** Four players form a square (8×8 or 10×10 yards, depending on age), with one or two "monkeys" in the middle.
- **How to Perform:**
    1. The outside players must keep the ball away from the defenders in the center.
    2. The goal is to play ***one-touch*** as much as possible.
    3. If a defender touches the ball or it goes out of bounds, the player who made the mistake switches to the middle.

✔ **The Secret:** Don't just pass to the player next to you. The "elite" move is the ***split pass***—passing right between the two defenders to the teammate on the opposite side.

2. The Multi-Ball Rectangle

This drill trains your "internal radar." It teaches you to track multiple threats at once.

- **The Setup:** Create 15 to 20 yards rectangle with 10–12 players inside.
- **How to Perform:**
    1. Everyone moves freely inside the rectangle.
    2. The coach introduces ***3 or 4 balls*** at the same time.
    3. Players must constantly pass and move, ensuring no ball ever stops moving and no two balls collide.

✔ **The Secret:** You must **scan** (look over your shoulder) before the ball arrives. If you only look at the ball coming toward you, you'll likely run into another player or a second ball.

3. "Further Leg" Passing

This is a technical rule applied to any basic passing line. It is the foundation of "body orientation."

- **The Setup:** Two players stand 10 meters apart.
- **How to Perform:**
    1. Player A passes the ball to Player B.
    2. Player B must receive the ball with their "further leg"—the foot furthest away from the ball.
    3. This forces your body to open up toward the rest of the field rather than closing off toward the passer.

✔ **The Secret:** By receiving with the further leg, your first touch automatically prepares you to see the whole pitch and make the next pass immediately.

4. The 3-Second Rule (Counter-Press)

In Barcelona's philosophy, the best time to win the ball back is the moment you lose it.

- **The Setup:** Any small-sided game (4v4 or 5v5).
- **How to Perform:**
    1. Play a normal match, but with one special rule:
    2. The moment your team loses possession, you have **exactly 3 seconds** to swarm the opponent and win it back.
    3. If you don't win it back in 3 seconds, you must immediately retreat into a defensive shape.

✔ **The Secret:** It's an "all-or-nothing" sprint. It's about the **mentality** of hunting the ball as a pack.

5. The Positional Game (Juego de Posición)

This is the most advanced drill at the academy. It teaches you that your "home" on the pitch is a zone, not a spot.

- **The Setup:** A large grid divided into vertical and horizontal lanes.
- **How to Perform:**
    1. Teams play a possession game, but players are restricted to their specific zones (like Wing, Half-space, or Center).
    2. **Rule of Three:** No more than three players can ever be in the same horizontal line.
    3. **Rule of Two:** No more than two players can be in the same vertical line.

✔ **The Secret:** If a teammate moves into your lane, you must move out of it. This creates constant *triangles* and ensures there is always a passing option available.

COACH'S CHALLENGE

Don't try to master all five at once. Pick the **Rondo** for your next practice. Focus on how many times you can "split" the defenders in the middle. That is where the magic begins.

The Origins of the Rondo

The Rondo was not "invented" in a single moment, but it was formalized at Barcelona by Laureano Ruiz, a legendary youth coach who arrived at the club in 1972. Ruiz was inspired by the patterns of play he saw in the great Hungarian teams of the 1950s.

Before Ruiz, training was often focused on physical fitness and long-distance running. Ruiz changed the philosophy to prioritize the ball, stating, "Everything that goes on in a match, except shooting, you can do in a rondo."

When Johan Cruyff returned to Barcelona as manager in 1988, he took Ruiz's warm-up drill and turned it into the central framework of the club's training methodology. Under Cruyff, it evolved from a "fun game" into a high-intensity technical and strategic tool.

GLOSSARY OF TERMS

The Language of La Masia

To play like a pro, you have to speak like one. Here are the key terms used in this chapter to describe the Barça style of play.

- ***The Scan:*** The act of looking over your shoulder before receiving the ball. This allows a player to know exactly where the defenders and teammates are located.
- ***Open Stance:*** Positioning your body so that your chest faces the field rather than the person passing you the ball. This is achieved by receiving with the further leg.
- ***Line-Breaking Pass:*** A pass that travels through or "splits" two defenders, effectively taking them out of the play.

- **Half-Space:** The vertical "corridor" on the pitch between the center and the wing. It is the most dangerous area for creative players like Lamine to operate.
- **Counter-Press:** An immediate, aggressive attempt to win the ball back within seconds of losing it, rather than dropping back to defend.
- **Joker (Neutral Player):** A player in a drill who always plays for the team in possession of the ball. This creates an "overload" (more attackers than defenders).
- **Body Orientation:** The direction your body is facing when the ball arrives. Good orientation allows you to make your next move in a single touch.
- **Passing Lane:** The clear path between two players. If a defender stands in the way, the lane is "closed."
- **Third Man Run:** A tactical move where Player A passes to Player B, who then passes to Player C, who has run into space. It is the hardest move for a defense to track.

THINK LIKE A PLAYER

- Which of these terms was new to you?
- The next time you play, can you count how many times you scan before your first touch?
- If you find yourself in the *half-space*, will you look for a dribble or a *line-breaking pass*?

WORDS TO REMEMBER

"In soccer, the eyes are just as important as the feet."

WHAT'S NEXT?

This book was about channeling Lamine's growth as a person and a player — and helping you shape your own journey. It's about seeing the game differently: thinking faster, moving smarter, and playing with confidence and joy. Remember, every great player starts somewhere, and it's the small choices you make every day that shape your game. Keep practicing, stay curious, support your teammates, and enjoy every moment on the pitch. The journey is yours — and it's only just beginning.

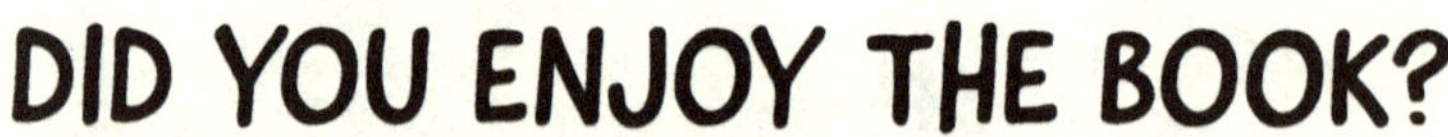

DID YOU ENJOY THE BOOK?

If your child enjoyed Play Like Lamine, we'd be grateful for a short Amazon review.

Your words help other parents and young players discover the book.

THE WORLD'S #1 BESTSELLING SOCCER SERIES!

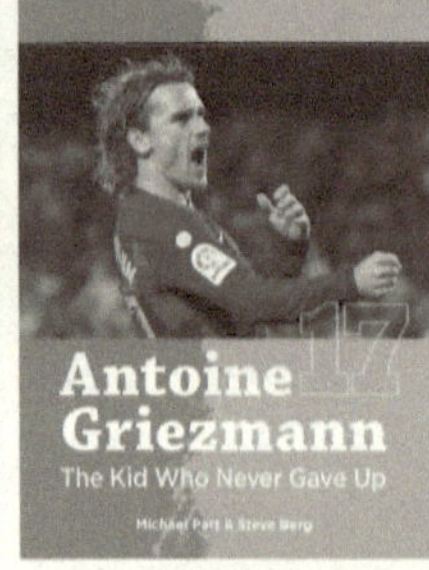

www.ingramcontent.com/pod-product-compliance
Lightning Source LLC
LaVergne TN
LVHW091010080826
845145LV00003B/1201

* 9 7 8 1 9 3 8 5 9 1 5 1 8 *